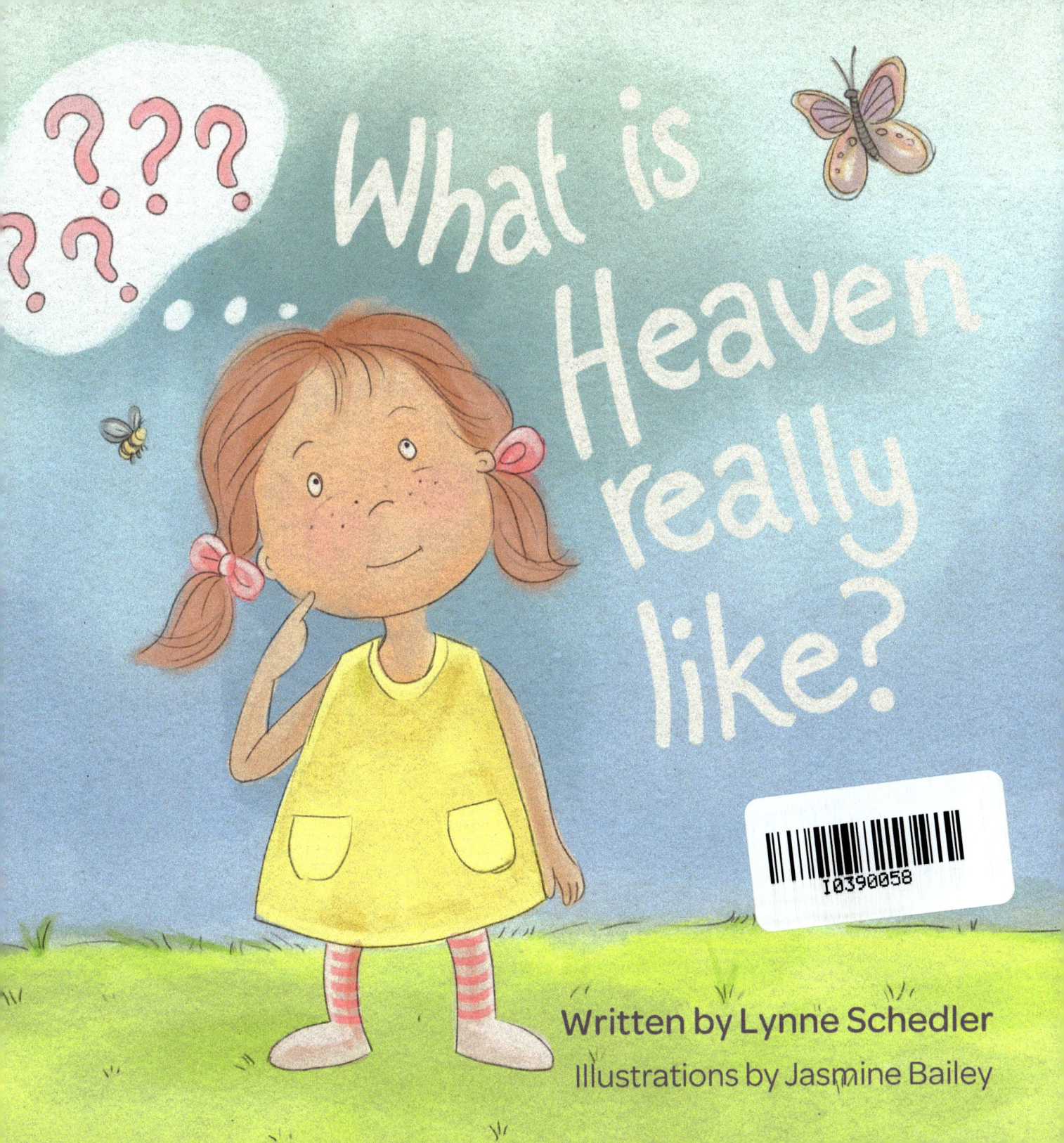

What Is Heaven Really Like?
Copyright ©2021 by Lynne Schedler
All rights reserved.

Illustrated by Jasmine Bailey
Interior Design by Inspire Books

No part of this publication may be reproduced, stored in a retrieval system, or transmitted in any form or by any means—electronic, mechanical, photocopy, recording, or any other—without the prior permission of the author.

Scripture quotations are from The ESV® Bible (The Holy Bible, English Standard Version®), copyright © 2001 by Crossway, a publishing ministry of Good News Publishers. Used by permission. All rights reserved.

Hardcover ISBN: 978-1-950685-76-9
Paperback ISBN: 978-1-950685-77-6
Library of Congress: 2021911704

Printed in the United States of America

I dedicate this book to Jesus.
Every line has been inspired by Him.

I would also like to dedicate this book to Lucas, a special little boy who recently lost his dear "Pappy."

I hope this book helps answer some of his—and other kids'—questions who are missing someone they love.

I pray that this book will be a blessing to you, and I hope to see you in heaven someday.

Hi, I'm Priscilla, and I want to know What is Heaven really like?

Heaven is filled with angels and Bible people too.
You will see your friends up there . . . some old and some new.

I wish I had wings so I could fly up to heaven.

"When the Son of Man comes in His glory, and all the angels with Him, then He will sit on His glorious throne."
Matthew 25:31

You'll find a river, the water of life, in which you can wade.
Heaven is a very safe place. You will never be afraid.

Then the angel showed me the river of the water of life, bright as crystal, flowing from the throne of God and of the Lamb.
Revelation 22:1

And I heard every creature in heaven and on earth and under the earth and in the sea, and all that is in them, saying, "To Him who sits on the throne and to the Lamb be blessing and honor and glory and might forever and ever!" And the four living creatures said, "Amen!" and the elders fell down and worshiped.
Revelation 5:13-14

I wonder if my dog Pogo is in heaven?

You will have a special house that Jesus built for you.
Animals galore are there, much more than in a zoo.

Heaven's gates are made of pearl. Jewels are sparkling on the walls.
We'll joyfully sing and praise our God, with dancing in the halls.

The foundations of the wall of the city were adorned with every kind of jewel. The first was jasper, the second sapphire, the third agate, the fourth emerald, the fifth sardonyx, the sixth sardius, the seventh chrysolite, the eight beryl, the ninth topaz, the tenth chrysoprase, the eleventh jacinth, and the twelfth amethyst.
Revelation 21:19-20

In Heaven you'll find a rainbow. It is all around God's throne.
With all the rejoicing multitudes, you'll never be alone.

*My favorite color of the rainbow is **purple!***

And He who sat there had the appearance of jasper and carnelian, and around the throne was a rainbow that had the appearance of an emerald.
Revelation 4:3

Pretty flowers grow everywhere,
all colors and all kinds,
More than in the crayon box that
you have left behind.

I really love to color! Maybe they have crayons in heaven?

Henceforth there is laid up for me the crown of righteousness, which the Lord, the righteous Judge, will award to me on that day, and not only to me but also to all who have loved His appearing.
2 Timothy 4:8

I wonder if it will be like my Barbie crown?

We will be given crowns to wear and robes of spotless white.

In heaven there will be no wrong and everything is right.

When can you go to heaven?
When Jesus comes or when you die.
Instantly, you'll be with God in that heavenly home on high.

For the Lord Himself will descend from heaven with a cry of command, with the voice of an archangel, and with the sound of the trumpet of God. And the dead in Christ will rise first. Then we who are alive, who are left, will be caught up together with them in the clouds to meet the Lord in the air, and so we will always be with the Lord. **1 Thessalonians 4:16-17**

And he said, "Jesus, remember me when You come into Your kingdom." And He said to him, "Truly, I say to you, today you will be with Me in paradise." **Luke 23:42-43**

How do you get to heaven? Angels come and take their flight.
They will carry you straight to God on wings of snowy white.

I'll get to see my grandpa again!

The poor man died and was carried by the angels to Abraham's side. The rich man also died and was buried.
Luke 16:22

Though eyes can't see, and ears can't hear, and minds can't know how it will be. God made for us an awesome place where we will spend eternity.

*But, as it is written,
What no eye has seen, nor ear heard, nor the heart of man imagined,
what God has prepared for those who love Him."*
1 Corinthians 2:9

Would you like to go to heaven?

God has a special place for you in this life, and in heaven. We can't get to heaven on our own goodness, so God made a special way for us. It's special because it's the only way that works.

We have all messed up at times, and that will keep us out of heaven. But God has a way so that your mess ups don't keep you out. He had a plan from the beginning of time to send His son, Jesus Christ, to die on the cross. Jesus' death finished the work that God wanted done to take away your mess ups forever. If you will receive His forgiveness, you will have a place in God's family and a home in heaven.

Pray this simple payer:

Jesus said, "Let the little children come to Me." I am coming to you now, Jesus, thanking you for forgiving all my mess ups. Come into my heart and make me a new person. God, You are now my heavenly Father, and Jesus is my Lord. Now I have the joy of being saved and knowing I will have a home in heaven with You one day. Thank you, Jesus. Amen

Some questions kids ask about heaven:

Is Jesus' mother, Mary, in heaven too?

Is there a rainbow in heaven?

When can you go to heaven?

What do you need to do to go to heaven?

Where is heaven?

What is in heaven?

How do you get to heaven?

What is it like in heaven?

Can people come back from heaven?

Is heaven above the clouds?

Do people in heaven know where we are?

Do our pets go to heaven?

I wonder what heaven is really like?

I trust that the pages in this book answer these questions and more for the children in your life.

Special Thanks...

To my friend, Donna, for sharing her grandson's story with me. Lucas was the inspiration behind, What is Heaven Really Like? *I hope this book will help answer his questions. I want to thank my grandson, Erick, for his assistance on the computer. He was a tremendous help to me.*

Meet the Author

Lynne Schedler is a wife, mother, and grandmother who lives in Florida with her family. Lynne grew up in Kansas City, Kansas, and moved with her family to Louisiana during her senior year of high school. There she met and married Richard, her husband of 54 years. They have one son and one grandson, who is 19.

Lynne loves animals; she and Richard have two Rat Terriers, Bolt and Chili, who are very special family members. Lynne gave her life to Jesus as a child in Bible School. She loves to write, especially poetry, and she also enjoys interior decorating.